جرَّةُ الفلّاح

مُنى نور الدّين

The Farmer's Jar

Levantine Arabic Reader – Book 7
(Lebanese Arabic)
by Mona Noureddine

lingualism

ISBN: 978-1-949650-50-1

Written by Mona Noureddine

Edited by Ahmed Younis and Matthew Aldrich

Cover art by Duc-Minh Vu

Audio by Serj D.

website: www.lingualism.com

email: contact@lingualism.com

Introduction

The **Levantine Arabic Readers** series aims to provide learners with much-needed exposure to authentic language. The books in the series are at a similar level (B1-B2) and can be read in any order. The stories are a fun and flexible tool for building vocabulary, improving language skills, and developing overall fluency. **This book is specifically Lebanese Arabic.**

The main text is presented on even-numbered pages with tashkeel (diacritics) to aid in reading, while parallel English translations on odd-numbered pages are there to help you better understand new words and idioms. A second version of the text is given at the back of the book, without the distraction of tashkeel and translations, for those who are up to the challenge.

New to this edition: the English translations have been revised for improved clarity and accuracy. Each story now also includes **20 comprehension questions** with example answers to help reinforce your understanding of the text. A **sequencing exercise** is provided as well, where you'll put ten key events from the story back in their correct order. These additions make the book even more useful for self-study, classroom use, or group discussions.

Visit www.lingualism.com/audio, to stream or download the free accompanying audio.

This book is also available in Modern Standard Arabic at www.lingualism.com/msar.

جرّةُ الفلّاح

بِضَيْعة صْغيرةٍ بالجّبل، كان في شابّ إسْمو ناجي، عايِش هُوَّ ومرْتو لَيال وبيّو.

بِهَيْدي الضّيْعة كانوا النّاس عايْشين حَياةْ بسيطة ومِتْواضْعة. بيزْرعوا أرْضُن ويخزّنُوا المونة لفصل الشّتي حتّى يِقْدروا يْعيشوا أيّام البرِد والتّلج. والنّاس بْهَيْدي الضّيْعة كان عِنْدُن قناعة بْطبيعةِ الحَياةْ بِالضّيْعة وكانوا عايْشين حَياتُن التقْليدية مَبْسوطين.

بيّو لناجي كان كْتير يْحِبّ الأرْض. كان عِنْدو بُسْتان دِرة[1] بْيِهْتمّ فيه كْتير. هَيْدا البِسْتان كان مصْدر العَيْش للْعَيْلة كِلّا.

بيّو لناجي بْآخِر فترْة مِن عُمْرو مِرِض كْتير، لحدّ ما في نهار كان وَضْعو الصّحّي كْتير مِتْدهْور.

عيّط لإبْنو ناجي حتّى يْخبّرو بوصيتو قبل ما يْموت وقلّو: "ناجي يا إبْني، أنا وَضْعي الصّحّي كْتير عم يِتْدهْوَر وحاسِس إنّو يِمْكِن هَيْدي تْكون آخِر أيّام حَياتي. كِرْمال هيْك بدّي وَصّيك يا إبْني إنّو تِهْتمّوا بْبعْض إنتَ ولَيال في حال أنا مِتِت، وما تِنْسوا تِهْتمّوا بالبِسْتان. هَيْدا البِسْتان بيعْنيلي كْتير.

The Farmer's Jar

In a small mountain village, there was a young man named Naji, living with his wife Layal and his father.

In that village, people lived a simple and modest life. They cultivated their land and stored food preserves for the winter so they could survive the cold and snow. The people in that village were content with the nature of village life and lived their traditional lives happily.

Naji's father loved the land deeply. He had a cornfield that he cared for very much. That cornfield was the family's main source of livelihood.

Toward the end of his life, Naji's father became very ill—until one day, his health deteriorated severely.

He called his son Naji to share his final wishes before he died and told him, "Naji, my son, my health is getting much worse, and I feel that these may be the last days of my life. That's why I want to ask you, my son, to take care of each other—you and Layal—if I die. And don't forget to take care of the cornfield. That field means a lot

---

¹ Pronunciation of many words varies from region to region. The word for 'corn' can be pronounced ذرة, ذُرة, and even ذرَة. You may notice the narrator (on the audio track) uses the first two pronunciations interchangeably through the story.

قضّيت كِلّ حَياتي عم بِزْرعو وعِشْنا كِلّ هالعُمُر مِنّو. وهَيْدا البِسْتان ورِتْتو مِن جِدّك بسّ كِنْت شابّ بِعُمْرك وهلّأ عم وَرَّثْتك ياه لإلك. اِعْتِني فيه وما تْخَلّيه يِتْبهْدل لإنّ هالبِسْتان رح يْكون مَصْدر عَيْشك الوَحيد إنْتَ ومرْتك لَيال ورح يْأمِّنْلْكُن أكِل لفصْل الشِّتي."

تاني يوْم الصُّبْح فاق ناجي ولقى بيّو ميِّت. زِعِل عْلَيْه كْتير وصاروا هُوّ ولَيال وَحيدين مِن دون وُجود بيّو. ما في غيْرُن وغيْر بِسْتان الدّرة يَلّي ورَتّو ياه بيّو كِرْمال يْعيش مِنّو هُوّ ومرْتو.

بِسْتان الدّرة يَلّي ورِتْتو ناجي ولَيال كان يَعْطي محْصول كْتير كْبير، بيكفّيْن مونِة لكِلّ السِّنة. بسّ مع الوَقْت، ناجي ما كان يِهْتمّ بالبِسْتان وما كان يِعْتِني بِشتْل الدّرة. لهيْك مِن بعْد سِنِة مِن موْت بيّو صار محْصود البِسْتان يِتْراجِع بْشكْل كْتير كْبير ويْقِلّ عدد الدّرة يَلّي فيه، لَوَقِت بطّلوا لَيال وناجي يْكَفّيْهُن لحتّى ياكْلوا ويْخزّنوا مونِة لفصْل الشِّتي.

لَيال ما كانِت تْحِبّ الشِغِل وكانْت كْتير تْنِقّ على ناجي كِرْمال يِشْتِغِل بِالأرْض ويِهْتمّ فيا، بسّ ناجي كان كِسْلان وما كان مِهْتمّ بالزّراعة أبداً. كان كِلّ الوَقِت عم يِشْكي مِن زراعِةْ الأرْض ومِن الشِّغِل فيا.

to me. I spent my whole life growing it, and we've lived off it all these years. I inherited it from your grandfather when I was your age, and now I'm passing it on to you. Take care of it and don't let it go to waste, because this field will be your only source of income for you and your wife Layal. It will provide your food for the winter."

The next morning, Naji woke up and found that his father had died. He was deeply saddened, and now he and Layal were left alone without his father. It was just the two of them and the cornfield his father had passed down to him, which they had to rely on for their livelihood.

The cornfield that Naji and Layal inherited used to yield a very large harvest—enough to provide for them for the entire year. But over time, Naji stopped caring for the field and neglected the corn plants. So after a year had passed since his father's death, the field's yield had declined drastically. There were fewer and fewer corn stalks, until Naji and Layal no longer had enough to eat or to store food for the winter.

Layal didn't like working and constantly nagged Naji to work the land and take care of it, but Naji was lazy and not interested in farming at all. He kept complaining all the time about working the land and how much he disliked it.

وبْنفْس الوَقِت لَيَال ما كانِت تْساعِد ناجي وكانِت بسّ تُطْلُب مِنّو هُوّ يِهْتمّ بِالبِسْتان، لحدّ ما بِقي البِسْتان مِن دون اِهْتِمام مِن قِبِل حدن وصارِت حالِةْ البِسْتان كِلّ يوْم أسْوأ مِن يوْم.

في نهار كانِت لَيَال كْتير مْعصّبِة مِن الوَضِع ومِن قِلِّةْ المحْصول، وصارِت كْتير تِشْكي مِن ناجي ومِن عدم اِهْتِمامو بِالأرْض.

وناجي كان كِلّ الوَقِت مِلْتِهي بِالتِّلِفوْن والإنْترْنت، لحدّ ما بلّشِت لَيَال تْلِحّ بِالطّلب على ناجي وقالِتْلو: "شيل هالتِّلِفوْن مِن إيدك وحاجِة تْضيِّع وَقْتك على الإنترْنت واللِّعب! قوم اِهْتمّ شْوَيّ بِهالبِسْتان أحْسن ما بُكْرا نْموت مْن الجّوع!"

ناجي ضحِك ضِحْكِة بِاسْتِهْزاء وردّ عْلَيَا وقالّا: "إنْتي مِفْتِكْرة إنّو المِشْكِلِة مِنّي؟ إنّو إذا أنا هلأ لْعِبت بِالتِّلِفوْن بْيِبِس البِسْتان؟ نِحْنا ما إلْنا حظّ بْهالبِسْتان ولَوْ بِدّو يَعْطينا محْصول زْيادِة كان عطانا. هَيْدا البِسْتان مِنْحوس، ما بِدّي ضيِّع وَقْتي بِالشِّغِل فيه." ورِجِع ناجي حِمِل تِلِفوْنو وبلّش يِلْعب عْلَيْه.

[3:32]

At the same time, Layal didn't help Naji either—she would only tell him to take care of the field. So eventually, the field was left without any attention from anyone, and its condition kept getting worse by the day.

One day, Layal was extremely frustrated with the situation and with how little the field was producing. She started complaining a lot about Naji and how he wasn't taking care of the land.

Meanwhile, Naji was always busy with his phone and the internet, until Layal started pushing him harder and said, "Put that phone down and stop wasting your time on the internet and playing games! Get up and take care of the field, or we're going to starve to death soon!"

Naji laughed mockingly and replied, "You really think it's my fault? That the field is dying just because I'm playing on my phone? We just have no luck with this field. If it were going to give us more crops, it would've already. This field is cursed—I'm not wasting my time working on it." Then he picked up his phone again and continued playing.

نْزعجِت لَيال مْن الرَّدّ تبع ناجي ومِن عدم مُبالاتو بالشِّغل بالأرْض وبِتحْسين وَضْع البِسْتان، وقالِتلو بانْزِعاج: "إنْتَ هَيْدا يَلّي شاطِر فيه، تْشيل اللّوْم عن حالك وما تتْحمّل المسْؤولية. مْقضّى كِلّ وَقْتك عَ التِّلِفوْن لِعْب وسوْشال مِيدْيا وتضْييع وَقت عَ الفاضي. لَوْ إنّك سقَيْت البِسْتان وهْتمّيْت فيه مْنيح كان هلّأ عطانا محْصول أكْتر وكِنّا أمّنّا مونة يَلّي بِتْكِفينا لفصْل الشِّتي وما كِنّا تْبهْدلْنا. بُكْرا بفصْل الشِّتي شو بدّنا ناكُل؟ مِن وَيْن بدّنا نْجيب طْحين وخبِز في حال ما قْدِرْنا هلّأ نِتْموّن مِن محْصول البِسْتان؟"

بسّ فِعْلِياً المِشْكْلِة ما كانت مِن البِسْتان مِتِل ما ناجي قال. المِشْكْلِة كانت إنّو ناجي ولَيال ما كانوا عم يِهْتمّوا بالبِسْتان وكان ناجي كِلّ الوَقت يِلْعب على التِّلِفوْن ويْقضّي كِلّ النّهار على السّوْشال مِيدْيا والإنْترنت، ولَيال تِشْكي مِن ناجي مِن دون ما هِيِّ تِشْتِغِل كمان بالبِسْتان. لهَيْدا السّبب البِسْتان بطّل يَعْطينُ حصاد مِتِل ما كان يَعْطينُ مِن قبِل.

بسّ لَيال ضلّت تْنِقّ على ناجي وتِشْكي مِن تصرُّفاتو بالبيت لوَقْت طَويل، لحدّ ما نْزعج مِنا ومْن الحديث وبطّل قادِر يِتْحمّل مُلاحظاتا، وقالّا:

[4:59]

Layal was upset by Naji's response and his lack of interest in working the land or improving the condition of the field. She said to him, clearly annoyed, "This is what you're good at—blaming anything but yourself and refusing to take responsibility. You spend all your time on your phone, playing games and scrolling social media, wasting time for nothing. If you had watered the field and taken proper care of it, we would've had a better harvest by now and would've been able to store food for the winter. We wouldn't be in this mess. What are we going to eat when winter comes? Where are we going to get flour and bread if we don't stock up now from what the field gives us?"

But in reality, the problem wasn't the field like Naji claimed. The real issue was that neither Naji nor Layal was taking care of it. Naji spent all his time playing on his phone and scrolling social media and the internet, while Layal just kept complaining about Naji without working in the field either. That's why the field stopped producing crops like it used to.

Still, Layal kept nagging Naji and complaining about his behavior at home for a long time—until he got fed up and couldn't handle her

"شو بدّك ياني أَعْمُل طيِّب؟ أصْلاً البْسْتان ما في مَحْصول والدّرة المَوْجود ما بْيعِمِلنا شي وأكيد ما بْيِكْفينا بالشِّتي، يَعْني إذا حصدْناهُن أوْ لأ هِيِّ ذاتا لإنّ الكميّة كْتير قليلة."

جاوَبِتو لَيال وقالِتْلو: "قوم نْزال جيب الدّرة المَوْجود حتّى لَوْ قْلال، واسْقي الشّتْلات الصُّغار بلْكي الشّهْر الجاي بيكْبر وبيزيد المَحْصول شْوَيّ قِبل ما يوصل فصْل الشِّتي. بيضَلّ أحْسن مِن اللِّعب وتِضْييع الوَقِت على التِّلفوْن."

ناجي نْزِعج مِن مُلاحظات لَيال الكْتيرة وقرّر يِنْزل على البِسْتان كِرْمال تْوَقِّف الجِّدال معو حَوْل هَيْدا المَوْضوع. أخد جرّة كان جايِبا جْديد ونِزِل كِرْمال يْعبّي فِيا الدُّرة.

وَقْت وِصِل على البِسْتان شاف إنّو الدُّرة المَوْجود قليل كْتير وما بيعبّي كَعْب الجرّة حتّى. لهيْك قرّر يِرْجع عَ البيْت مِن دون ما يْجيب الدّرة ومِن دون ما يِهْتمّ بالبِسْتان، وكان بْحالة نفْسية كْتير تِعْبانة لإنّ ما عارِف مِنّيْن بدّو يأمِّن الأكِل والشّرِب للبيْت.

comments anymore. He snapped and said, "What do you want me to do, huh? The field barely has any crops, and the corn we do have won't do us any good—it's not enough for the winter. Whether we harvest it or not, it's the same—it's way too little."

Layal replied, "Just go and pick what corn there is, even if it's a small amount. And water the young plants—maybe by next month the crop will grow a little more before winter comes. That's still better than sitting around playing on your phone and wasting time."

Annoyed by Layal's constant remarks, Naji decided to go down to the field just to put an end to the argument. He took a new jar they had bought and headed out to fill it with corn.

When he got to the field, he saw that the amount of corn was very small—barely enough to even cover the bottom of the jar. So he decided to return home without bringing any corn and without doing anything in the field. He was in a very bad mood because he had no idea how he was going to provide food and water for the house.

هُوّ وراجِع مِن البِسْتان، سِمِع صَوْت كْتير غريب طالِع مِن قَلْب الجرّة وعم بيقِلّو بِصوْت واطي وهادي: "رْجاع على البِسْتان يا ناجي وحْصود الدُّرة المَوْجود. حتّى لَوْ كان في بسّ حبّة وِحْدِة أفْضل مِن إنّك تِتْرِكا. مُمْكِن يِجي يَوْم وتِعْتاز تاكُل حبّةْ دُرة وَحْدِة."

ناجي سْتغْرب الصَّوْت وخاف كْتير. وصار يْدوِّر كِرْمال يَعْرِف كيف طِلِع هَيْدا الصَّوْت مِن قَلْب الجرّة. وصار يِتْطلّع بِقَلْب الجرّة تَيْشوف إذا فِيا شي، بسّ الجرّة كانِت فاضْية.

بِالأخير فكّر حالو عم يِتْخايَل الصَّوْت مِن راسو وإنّو الصَّوْت مِش حقيقي. بسّ بِنفْس الوَقِت قرّر يِسمع لِهيْدا الصَّوْت الجايي مِن الجرّة ورجِع عَ البِسْتان كِرْمال يْجيب الدُّرة.

بسّ رِجِع ناجي عَ البِسْتان، قطَف الدُّرة المَوْجود وحطّن بِالجرّة، وكانوا الدُّرة كْتير قْلال وما عبّوا غيْر شْوَيّ مِن كعْب الجرّة.

هُوّ وعم بيعبّي وِقِع مِنّو محْبسو الدّهب ونِزِل بِقَلْب الجرّة. وفجْأة شاف ناجي كِلّ حبّات الدُّرة يَلّي بِالجرّة عم تِلْمع وتْحوّلوا لدهب.

[8:20]

As he was walking back from the field, Naji heard a very strange sound coming from inside the jar. A soft, calm voice said to him, "Go back to the field, Naji, and harvest the corn that's there. Even if there's only a single cob, it's better than leaving it behind. A day might come when you'll need to eat just one kernel of corn."

Naji was confused by the voice and got very scared. He started looking around, trying to figure out how the sound was coming from inside the jar. He looked into the jar to see if there was anything inside, but it was empty.

In the end, he thought he was imagining the voice—that it was all in his head and not real. But at the same time, he decided to listen to the voice coming from the jar and went back to the field to collect the corn.

When Naji returned to the field, he picked the remaining corn and placed it into the jar. There were very few cobs, and they only covered a small part of the bottom of the jar.

While he was filling the jar, his gold ring slipped off and fell into it. Suddenly, Naji saw all the corn cobs in the jar start to glow—they turned into gold.

ورجِع سِمع نَفْس الصَّوْت عم يِحْكيه مِن قلْب الجرّة مرّة تانْية، وقلّو: "بِما إنّك قرّرْت تِرْجع وتِشْتِغِل بِالأرْض وتُقْطُف الدُّرة، هَيْدي الدُّرة تْحوّلِت لدهب. وصار فيك إنْتَ ومرْتك تْبيعوهُن وتْعيشوا حَياةْ كريمة مِن دون ما تِعْتازوا حدن. بسْ تْذكّر مْنيح إنّو ما لازِم حدا يعْرِف بِهَيْدا الشّي، وهَيْدا لازِم يْضلّ سِرّ بَيْناتْنا، وفي حال طْمُعْت وصار بدّك تْخبّي المصاري يَلّي منّك بِحاجِتا رح تْحِلّ عليْك وعلى مرْتك لعْنِةْ الجرّة."

ناجي نْبسط كْتير وكْتشف إنّو هَيْدي الجرّة سِحْرية. بسْ رِجِع عَ البيْت، أخد قرار يِسْمع نصيحْةْ الجرّة وما يْخبِّر حدن بالمَوْضوع، ولا حتّى مرْتو لَيال.

وقلّا للجرّة: "بوعْدِك إنّو ما رح نِطْمع ورح نِكْتِفي بِالقدِر يَلّي نِحْنا بِحاجة لإلو كِرْمال نْعيش وما نْكون بِحاجِة. أكْتر مِن هيْك ما رح أطْلُب منّك وما رح إسْعى لَيْكون عِنْدي دهب كْتير. كِلّ هدفي كون عم أمِّن أكْل وشِرِب للبيْت لإنّ مِن بعْد ما مات بيّي بطّل عِنْدي حدن والبِسْتان بطّل يَعْطينا محْصود كْفاية."

[9:57]

And once again, he heard the same voice speaking to him from inside the jar, saying, "Because you chose to come back, work the land, and harvest the corn, it has now turned into gold. Now you and your wife can sell it and live a dignified life without needing help from anyone. But remember this well: no one must know about this. It must remain a secret between us. And if you ever get greedy and start hiding money you don't actually need, the curse of the jar will fall upon you and your wife."

Naji was overjoyed and realized that the jar was magical. But when he got back home, he made the decision to follow the jar's advice and not tell anyone about it—not even his wife, Layal.

He said to the jar, "I promise that we won't be greedy and that we'll only take what we need to live without having to rely on anyone. I won't ask you for more, and I won't try to have too much gold. My only goal is to provide food and water for the house—because ever since my father died, I've had no one, and the field hasn't produced enough to support us."

بعْد فترْةْ أُسْبوع لاحظِت لَيال إنّو ناجي صار يْجيب غْراض على البيْت أكْتر مْن العادة، وسْتغْربِت منّيْن عم يْجيب المصاري لَيدْفع لكلّ هَيْدي الغْراض.

وضلِّت لَيال تِسْألو لناجي منّيْن عم يْجيب المصاري، بسّ هُوّ ما كان يْخبِّرا. وبلَيْلِة مِن اللَيالي ألحِّت لَيال على ناجي وضلِّت مُصِرّة إنّو تعْرِف الحقيقة.

ساعِتا ناجي قرّر يْخبِّرا بسّ طلب منّا ما تْخبِّر حدن. خبِّرا ناجي للَيال شو صار معو وعن قُصِّةْ الجرّة، وفرْجاها على الدُّرة يَلّي تْحوّلوا وصاروا دهب.

لَيال صارِت تِضْحك والفرْحة ما كانِت سايْعِتا، وقالِتْلو لناجي: "هَيْدي الجرّة رح تْكون وَسيلِتْنا لنْصير أغْنِيا ونِطْلع مِن حَياةْ الفُقُر يَلّي نِحْنا فِيا. رح نِشْتِري دُرة مْن السّوق نْبيعُن فِيا ونْحوِّلُن لدهب ونْبيعُن. بِهَيْدي الطّريقة منْصير أغْنِيا كْتير بِخِلال سِنِة، مِنِشْتِري قصْر كْبير وأرْض تانْية غيْر هَيْدي الأرْض ومْنِفْتح أكْبر مزرعة بِالبلد ومِنْتاجِر بِالمحْصول تبعا."

[11:37]

After a week, Layal noticed that Naji was bringing home more groceries and supplies than usual, and she was surprised—wondering where he was getting the money to pay for all of it.

She kept asking Naji where the money was coming from, but he wouldn't tell her. Then, one night, Layal pressed him hard and insisted on knowing the truth.

At that point, Naji decided to tell her—but he asked her not to tell anyone. Naji told Layal what had happened and about the story of the jar, and he showed her the corn that had turned into gold.

Layal started laughing, overjoyed, and said to Naji, "This jar is our way out—we're going to become rich and escape this life of poverty we've been living. We'll buy corn from the market, put it in the jar, turn it into gold, and sell it. That way, we'll become super rich within a year. We'll buy a big palace, more land than this one, start the biggest farm in the country, and trade in its crops!"

ناجي سْتغْرب ردِّةْ فِعِل مرْتو وخاف مْن الطّمع يَلّي شافو بعْيونا، وجاوَبا: "يِمْكِن ما لازِم نِطْمع كْتير يا لَيال، هَوْدي الدّهب بيعيْشونا سِنة ونِحْنا ما بحاجة لمصاري أكْتر مِن هيْك. المُهِمّ نِقْدر نْأمّن أكْلْنا وشِرْبْنا. شوفي وَضعْنا قبل هلّأ كيف كان وكيف صار. شو بدُّنا بزْيادِةْ المصاري إذا نِحْنا ما مِحْتاجينا؟"

لَيال ما قْتنعِت مِن ردِّةْ فِعِل ناجي وبِقْيِت مُصِرّة تِنْتْج أكْبر قدِر مُمْكِن مِن الدّهب مِن خِلال هَيْدي الجرّة، وردِّت عْلَيْه: "هَيْدي فُرْصِتْنا الدّهبية إنّو نْصير أغْنيا ونْجمِّع مصاري بيكفونا نْعيش كِلّ حَياتْنا بالنّعيم وبِقْصر بدل هالبيْت الصّغير يَلّي نِحْنا فيه. ما لازِم نْضيّع هَيْدي الفُرْصة مِن إيدْنا."

جاوَبا ناجي: "الجرّة وَقْتا حوّلِت الدُرة لدهب حِكْيِت معي وقالِتْلي إنّو قدّمِتْلْنا الدّهب لحتّى نِقْدر ناكُل ونْعيش، بسّ مِش لحتّى نْصير أغْنيا ونْتْرُك بَيْتنا. لهيْك ما لازِم نِطْمع ولازِم نِكْتِفي بالمَوْجود لإنّ في حال ما كْتفَيْنا رح تْحِلّ عْلَيْنا لعْنةْ الجرّة."

حاوَلِت لَيال تِقْنع ناجي بْفِكْرِتا بسّ هُوّ بِقي مُصِرّ إنّو ما لازِم يطْمعوا ولازِم يِكْتِفوا بالمَوْجود. لهيْك قرّر يِشْتِري بالدّهب دُرة وأكِل وشِرِب للبيْت.

[13:18]

Naji was surprised by his wife's reaction and became worried about the greed he saw in her eyes. He replied, "Maybe we shouldn't get too greedy, Layal. This gold can support us for a whole year, and we don't need more money than that. What matters is that we can secure our food and water. Just look at how things were before and how they are now. Why want more money if we don't actually need it?"

Layal wasn't convinced by Naji's response and remained determined to produce as much gold as possible through the jar. She replied, "This is our golden opportunity to become rich and collect enough money to live the rest of our lives in luxury—in a palace instead of this tiny house. We can't let this opportunity slip through our fingers."

Naji answered, "When the jar turned the corn into gold, it spoke to me and said that it gave us the gold so we could eat and live—not to become rich and abandon our home. That's why we shouldn't be greedy. We need to be content with what we have, because if we're not, the curse of the jar will fall upon us."

Layal tried to convince Naji of her plan, but he insisted that they shouldn't be greedy and should be content with what they had. So he decided to use the gold to buy corn and food and water for the household.

وكمان قرَّر إنّو يِسْتعْمِل الجرّة مرّة وحْدِة بالسِّنة في حال عْتازوا أكِل وما كان معْن مصاري كْفاية، بهَيْدي الطَّريقة ما بيكون أخلّ بِوَعْدو للجرّة.

بسّ لَيال ما حبّت الفِكْرة وما قْتنعت أبداً بمَوْقِف ناجي، وكان كلّ هدفا كيف بدّا تْصير غنية كْتير وصارِت تْفكّر كيف بدّا تاخُد الجرّة حتّى تعْمِل مِنا دهب ويْصير معا مصاري أكْتر.

بِلَيْلِة مْن اللَّيالي مِن عشية، فاتوا لَيال وناجي تْيْناموا. ولَيال ما قِدْرِت تْنام وكان راسا مشْغول بِالجرّة وبِالدّهب.

لهيْك بسّ نام ناجي، شافتو لَيال إنّو غِفي وإنّو مِش حاسِس عْلَيا، فقامِت لَيال بِاللّيْل وأخذِت الجرّة وخبّتا بالقبو تحْت البيت وحطَّت محلّا جرّة تانْية مِتْلا بالزّبط، وبِهَيْدي الطَّريقة ناجي ما رح يَعْرِف بالمَوْضوع ورح يْفكّر إنّو الجرّة الجْديدِة هيِّ نفْسا القديمة، وجرَّةْ الدّهب الحقيقية صارِت بإيد لَيال ومْخبّاية بالقبو مِن دون عِلِم ناجي.

تاني يَوْم راح ناجي على السّوق. باع الدّهب يَلّي معو وشْترى فيْن دُرة كِرْمال يِزْرع البِسْتان مِن جْديد، وشْترى كمان أكِل وشِرِب للبيْت.

[15:18]

He also decided that he would only use the jar once a year—if they ever needed food and didn't have enough money. That way, he wouldn't break the promise he made to the jar.

But Layal didn't like the idea and wasn't convinced at all by Naji's stance. Her only goal was to become very rich, and she began thinking about how to take the jar for herself and use it to make more gold.

One evening, Layal and Naji went to bed—but Layal couldn't sleep. Her mind was consumed with thoughts of the jar and the gold.

So when Naji fell asleep, Layal saw that he was out cold and wasn't aware of anything. She got up in the middle of the night, took the jar, and hid it in the cellar under the house. She replaced it with another jar that looked exactly the same. That way, Naji wouldn't notice anything and would think the new jar was the original one. The real gold jar was now in Layal's hands, hidden in the cellar without Naji's knowledge.

The next day, Naji went to the market. He sold the gold he had and used the money to buy corn seeds to replant the field, as well as food and drink for the house.

بسّ وِصِل ناجي، شافِت لَيال الدُّرة وشافِت وين ضبُّ كِرْمال تاني يَوْم يْقوم يِزْرعُن بِالبِسْتان.

بعْد نهار طَويل، فاتوا ناجي ولَيال مِتْل العادِة تْيْناموا، وبسّ نام ناجي بِاللّيْل أخدِت لَيال قِسِم مِن الدُّرة يَلّي شْتراهُن ونزْلِت على القبو.

فتحِت لَيال الجرّة وحطّت فيا الدُّرة ورِجْعِت حطّت محْبسا الدّهب فَوْقُن. نطرِت لَيال بِشغف تتْشوف كيف الدُّرة بدّو يْصير دهب.

وبِالفِعِل تْحوّلوا الدُّرة لدهب مِتِل ما صار أوّل مرّة مع ناجي. لَيال نْبسطِت كْتير إنّو خُطّتا نجحِت وصار معا دهب، وصار فيا تِشْتري درة أكْتر وتْحوّلُن لدهب.

وقالِت لنفْسا: "وأخيراً رح يِتْحقّق حِلْمي وصير غنية ويْصير معي كْتير مصاري. وأخيراً رح إشْتري قصِر كْتير كْبير وإطْلع مِن هالبيْت الصُّغير يَلّي عايْشة فيه."

نِسْيِت لَيال شو قلّا ناجي عن اللّعْنِة يَلّي معْقول تْصيبُن في حال طْمْعو، وكان كِلّ هدفا تِرْكيزا على كيف تعْمُل مصاري أكْتر.

[17:15]

When Naji got home, Layal saw the corn and noticed where he stored it so he could plant it in the field the next day.

After a long day, Naji and Layal went to bed as usual. But once Naji fell asleep, Layal took a portion of the corn he had bought and went down to the cellar.

She opened the jar, placed the corn inside, and then dropped her gold wedding ring on top of it. Layal waited eagerly to see if the corn would turn into gold.

And sure enough, the corn turned into gold—just like what had happened the first time with Naji. Layal was overjoyed that her plan had worked, and now she had gold. She could buy even more corn and turn that into gold too.

She said to herself, "Finally, my dream is coming true. I'm going to be rich and have so much money. I'm finally going to buy a huge palace and leave this small house I'm living in."

Layal had completely forgotten what Naji had told her about the curse that might befall them if they gave in to greed. All she could focus on was making more money.

لَيال صار معا دهب كْتير وضلِّت على مِدِّةْ شهِر تِشْتِري دُرة وتْحوِّلُن لدهب، مِن بَعْدا تْبيع الدّهب وتْخبّي المصاري بِخِزْنِة عِنْدا بالبِيَت.

بسّ هَيْدا الشّي ما ضلّ لَوَقْت كْتير، لإنّ بِيَوْم مِن الأيّام فات ناجي لعِنْد لَيال ونْتبهّ إنّو صِرْلا فترْة طَويلِة ما لابْسِة محْبس الدّهب تبعا، وسْتغْرب كْتير المَوْضوع لإنّ لَيال كانِت كِلّ حَياتا مِن بعْد الزّواج تِلْبُس محْبس الدّهب وما تِشْلحو مِن إيدا.

كِرْمال هيْك سألا ناجي للَيال: "وِيْن محْبسك الدّهب يَلّي كِنْتي دايْماً تِلْبْسيه؟ صِرْلِك فترْة طَويلِة ما لابْسْتيه، ضابِتْيه بِشي مطْرح بالبِيَت؟"

تْلبِّكِت لَيال مْن السُّؤال وما عِرْفِت كيف تْجاوِب، وصارْت تْجرِّب تْأَلِّف حِجج ومُبرِّرات حتّى ناجي ما يَعْرِف بالقُصّة المزْبوطة حَوْل جرِّة الدّهب يَلّي خبِّتا لَيال بِالقبو.

وجاوبِتو لَيال لناجي وقالت: "ما بعْرِف وَيْن بالزِّبِط ضيِّعْتو. كان بإيدي مِن فترْة بسّ ما بعْرِف كيف ضاع. فجْأة فِقِت مْن النّوْم وتْطلّعِت بإيدي ولقَيْت المحْبس ضاع. يمْكِن وِقِع بالأرْض أَوْ بالمطبخ، ويمْكِن ضاع بالبِسْتان، ما بعْرِف وَيْن مَوْجود. وما كِنت لاقيه. بسّ إنْتَ ما تِعْتِل همّ. بُكْرا مِنْلاقيه مِش مِشْكْلِة. ما كْتير تْفكّر بالمَوْضوع."

[18:55]

Layal kept turning corn into gold for a whole month. She would buy corn, transform it into gold, then sell the gold and stash the money in a safe she kept in the house.

But that didn't last long. One day, Naji walked in on Layal and noticed that she hadn't worn her gold wedding ring for quite some time. He was surprised, because Layal had always worn it ever since they got married—she never took it off.

So Naji asked Layal, "Where's your gold ring—the one you always wear? It's been a while since I've seen you wearing it. Did you stash it somewhere in the house?"

Layal got flustered by the question and didn't know how to respond. She started scrambling to come up with excuses and justifications so Naji wouldn't find out the truth about the gold jar she had hidden in the cellar.

Layal answered Naji and said, "I don't really know where I lost it. I had it on recently, but I don't know how it disappeared. I just woke up one day, looked at my hand, and the ring was gone. Maybe it fell on the ground or in the kitchen—or maybe I lost it in the field, I really don't know. But don't worry. We'll find it eventually—it's not a big deal. Don't think too much about it."

لَيال كانِت كْتير مْلبّكِة هِيٍّ وعم بِنْجاوْبو لناجي وما عِرْفِت تِحْكي مْنيح، وصارِت تِتْلبّك بِالحكي وصار وِجّا أحمر مِن خَوْفا إنّو ناجي يَعْرِف بِالحقيقة.

ناجي نْتبه ولاحظ إنّو في شي غريب صايِر وإنّو لَيال عم تْخبّي شي عنّو، وحسّ إنّو لَيال ما كانِت عم تْقول الحقيقة عن قُصّةُ المحْبس.

مِن بعْدا، قرّر ناجي يْراقِب لَيال بِالسِّرّ مِن دون ما تْحسّ عْلَيْه كِرْمال يِكْتِشِف شو مْخبّية عنّو.

ومِتِل كِلّ يَوْم، كانِت لَيال تُنْطُر ناجي لَيْفوت يْنام كِرْمال تِنْزل هِيٍّ عَ القبو وتْحوِّل الدُّرة لدهب، وتْبيعْن وتْخبّي المصاري بِخزْنِة خبّتا على تِتْخيتِةْ المطْبخ.

وبْلَيْلِة مِن اللَّيالي فاتوا لَيال وناجي كِرْمال يْناموا، بسّ ناجي قرّر هالمرّة إنّو يْمثّل على لَيال ويَعْمِل حالو نايِم، لأنّو حسّ إنّو لَيال ما عم بِتْنام قبِل ما هُوِّ يِغْفى.

[20:59]

Layal was extremely flustered while answering Naji. She was stumbling over her words, and her face turned red out of fear that Naji would discover the truth.

Naji noticed that something was off. He sensed that Layal was hiding something from him and that she wasn't telling the truth about the missing ring.

After that, Naji decided to secretly keep an eye on Layal without her noticing, to find out what she was hiding from him.

Just like every day, Layal waited for Naji to fall asleep so she could sneak down to the cellar, turn corn into gold, sell it, and hide the money in a safe she had hidden under the kitchen floorboards.

One night, Naji and Layal went to bed as usual—but this time, Naji decided to pretend to fall asleep, because he had a feeling Layal never went to bed until she was sure he was asleep.

ناجي عِمِل حالو نايِم وصار يُراقِب تحرُكات لَيال تَيْشوف شو رح تعْمُل مِن بعْدا. مِن بعْد ١٠ دقايِق، وبسّ شافِت لَيال إنّو ناجي نام، قامِت مِن التّخِت بالسّرّ مِن دون ما تعْمِل أيّ صَوْت أوْ ضجّة ونزِلِت مِتْل العادِة على القبو كِرْمال تْحوّل الدُّرة لدهب.

هِيّ ونازْلِة على القبو حسّ علَيَا ناجي وقام مْن التّخِت ولِحِقا مِن دون ما تْحِسّ عْلَيْه، ونزِل وَراها على القبو يَلّي تحِت بَيْتُن.

فتح ناجي باب القبو فتْحة صْغيرِة مِن دون ما يَعْمِل ضجّة أوْ صَوْت، وشاف إنّو لَيال مْخبية الجرّة بالقبو وعم تْحوّل الدُّرة لدهب بِشكِل سِرّي مِن دون ما حدا يَعْرِف بالمَوْضوع. ناجي نْزعج وخاف كْتير مِن إنّو تْحِلّ عْلَيْن لعْنِةْ الجرّة، وتْذكّر الحكي يَلّي قالِتْلو ياه الجرّة بأوّل مرّة حوّل فِيا الدُّرة لدهب.

فتح الباب وفات وقِف حدّ لَيال وقلّا: "لَيال شو عم تعْمْلي هون؟ مِش على أساس كِنْتي نايْمِة؟ شو نْزِلْتي تعْمْلي بالقبو بِهَيْدا الوَقْت المِتأخّر مْن اللّيْل؟ وهَيْدا شو يَلّي حدِّك؟" وأشار بإيدو على الجرّة.

[22:35]

Naji pretended to be asleep and watched Layal to see what she would do. After about ten minutes, when Layal thought Naji was asleep, she quietly got out of bed without making a sound and snuck down to the cellar like she usually did to turn corn into gold.

As she headed to the cellar, Naji got up from bed and followed her without her noticing. He went down after her to the cellar underneath their house.

Naji opened the cellar door just slightly, silently, and saw that Layal had hidden the jar down there and was secretly turning corn into gold without anyone knowing. Naji was upset and deeply afraid that the curse of the jar would fall upon them. He remembered exactly what the jar had told him the first time it had turned corn into gold.

He pushed open the door and stepped into the cellar, stood beside Layal, and said, "Layal, what are you doing down here? Weren't you supposed to be asleep? What are you doing in the cellar at this late hour? And what's that next to you?"—he pointed at the jar.

بسّ سِمْعِت لَيال ناجي عم يِحْكِيَا برمِت وشافِتو واقِف حدّا. نِقْزِت لَيال وتْفاجِئِت مِن وُجود ناجي بِالقبو، لِإنّ كِلّ فِكْرا إنّو ناجي كان نايِم وما شافا نِزْلِت، مِن بعْدا برمِت لَيال بِسِرْعة كْبيرة وكان بَدا تْخبّي الجرّة وَراها كِرْمال ناجي ما يْشوفا.

ومِن كِتْر السّرْعة بِالحركِة والارْتِباك مْن المَوْقف يَلّي صار معا، ضرَبِت لَيال إجْرا بِالجرّة وزحطِت ووقْعِت جُوّاتا وصارِت تُطْلُب المُساعدِة مِن ناجي.

ركض ناجي لعِنْدا كِرْمال يْساعِدا تِطْلَع مِن قلْب الجرّة، وفجْأة بِيلاقي إنّو لَيال تْحوّلِت لدهب وصارِت جماد وبطّل فِيا تِتْحرّك. كان بعْدا قادْرة بسّ تِحْكي.

ناجي خاف كْتير مِن الشّي يَلّي صار مع لَيال وبلّش يْجرّب يْلاقي طريقة كيف مُمْكِن تِرْجع لَيال لحالِتا الطّبيعية، بسّ للأسف ما قِدِر يِعْمِل أي شي لِأنّ لَيال تْحوّلِت لدهب.

مرّة جْديدة بيطْلَع الصَّوْت نفسو مِن قلْب الجرّة، بسّ هَيْدي المرّة كان غاضِب ومزْعوج كْتير مِن تصرُّفات ناجي ولَيال، وقلّا للَيال: "طمعِك يا لَيال خلّاكي توقعي بِالجرّة وتِتْحوّلي لدهب، وهلّا ما بقى يِنْفعِك كِلّ

[24:33]

When Layal heard Naji speaking to her, she turned around and saw him standing next to her. She jumped in shock, surprised to find Naji in the cellar—she had thought he was asleep and didn't see her sneak out. She quickly turned around, trying to hide the jar behind her so Naji wouldn't see it.

But in her rush and panic, Layal accidentally kicked the jar, slipped, and fell inside it. She started calling out to Naji for help.

Naji rushed to help her out of the jar, but suddenly saw that Layal had turned into gold. She had become a lifeless object—unable to move, though she could still speak.

Naji was terrified by what had happened to Layal and began trying to find a way to return her to normal. But unfortunately, he couldn't do anything—Layal had turned into gold.

Once again, the same voice came from the jar—but this time, it was angry and deeply upset by the actions of Naji and Layal. It said to Layal, "Your greed, Layal, caused you to fall into the jar and turn

المصاري يَلّي خَبَّيْتِيا. ما كنْفَيْني بِالقليل وصار بدّك تْراكْمي ثْرْوِتِك وتِجْمعي مصاري منّك بِحاجة لإلا. هلّا صِرْتي إنْتي بِنفْسِك دهب، والطَّريقة الوَحيدة لإنّك تِرْجعي مِتِل ما كِنْتي مِن قبِل، هيِّ إنّو تْقْضي كِلّ بقيِةْ عُمْرِك عم تِزْرعي دُرة وتْوَزِّعِينُ على النّاس الفُقرا والمِحْتاجين، وفي حال مرق نْهار واحد مِن دون ما تْساعْدي فيه النّاس، رح تِرْجعي لدهب. وبِنفْس الوَقِت كِلّ المصاري يَلّي خَبَّيْتِيا بِالخِزْنِة رح تِخْتِفي، وكِلّ الدّهب يلّي خبّيْتِيه رح يِتْحوّل مرّة جْديدِة لدُرة."

وكمان حِكْيِت الجرّة مع ناجي وقالِتْلو: "وإنْتَ يا ناجي، وَعِدِتْني إنّك ما رح تْخبِّر حدن وما رح تِطْمعوا بِالدّهب، ورْجِعِت خبّرْت لَيال وصار بدّا تعْمُل مصاري أكْتر مِن حاجِتا. هَيْدا يَلّي صار بِمرْتِك لَيال هُوّ لعْنِةْ الجرّة يَلّي خبّرْتِك عنّا وحذرْتِك منّا. هلّا حلّ المِشْكِلِة صار بَين إيدَيْكُن وإنْتو رح تِدْفعوا تمن الأخْطاء يَلّي عْمِلْتوها."

ناجي ولَيال ما كان عِنْدُن خَيار تاني غيرْ إنّو تِقْبل لَيال بِهَيْدي الشّروط يَلّي قالِتْلا هيِّ الجرّة، أوْ بْتِضلّا كِلّ بقيةْ عُمْرا قُطْعِةْ دهب ما فِيا تِتْحرّك وما فِيا تِمْشي.

وافِقِت لَيال على شُروط الجرّة، ورِجْعِت لطبيعِتا وخْتفى الدّهب عن جِسْما وصار فِيا تِتْحرّك.

into gold. And now, all the money you hid won't help you. You weren't content with what you had—you wanted to pile up wealth and gather money you didn't even need. Now *you* have become gold. The only way to return to your human form is to spend the rest of your life planting corn and distributing it to the poor and needy. And if even a single day passes without you helping others, you will turn back into gold. Also, all the money you hid in the safe will disappear, and all the gold you hoarded will turn back into corn."

Then the jar spoke to Naji and said, "And you, Naji—you promised me that you wouldn't tell anyone and that you wouldn't be greedy for gold. But you told Layal, and she ended up wanting more money than she needed. What happened to your wife Layal is the curse of the jar, the one I warned you about. Now the solution is in your hands, and you both must pay the price for the mistakes you made."

Naji and Layal had no other option. Layal had to accept the conditions the jar gave her—or else remain a lifeless golden statue, unable to move or live.

Layal agreed to the jar's conditions, and she returned to her natural form. The gold vanished from her body, and she could move again.

وضلّت لَيال كلّ حَياتا عم تِشْتِغِل مع زَوْجا ناجي بِالبِسْتان وتْساعِد النّاس المِحْتاجِة، وتْعلّمِت لَيال درس إنّو ما لازِم تْزيد طمعا ولازِم تِرْضى بِحاجاتا مِن دون ما تِطْمَع أكْتر.

وناجي صار يِهتمّ أكْتر بِالبِسْتان لأنّ الجرّة ما عاد تعْطيْنُ دهب مِن بعْد يَلّي عمِلتو لَيال، وصاروا مجبورين يِرْجعوا يِزْرعوا الأرْض ويحصْدوها حتّى يِقْدروا يْعيشوا ويْنفّذوا شُروط الجرّة ويْساعْدوا النّاس الفُقرا.

مع الوَقِت وبعْد أكْتر مِن سِنِة، رِجْعِت الحَياةْ والخضار على البِسْتان ورِجِع المحْصود يْزيد ويِكْتر، وصاروا لَيال وناجي كلّ يَوْم يِهْتمّوا بِالأرْض ويعْتِنوا فيا ويحُصْدوا الحصاد، وصار البِسْتان أكْبر بِكْتير وتْحوّل مِن بِسْتان صْغير، لمصْدر عيش عدد كْبير مْن العيّل المِحْتاجِة بِالضّيْعة.

وكْتشفوا لَيال وناجي إنّو صارِت حَياتُنْ سعيدِة أكْتر مِن قبل وصارِت علاقتُنْ بِالنّاس يَلّي عم يْساعْدوهُنْ أقْوى، وكلّ الضّيْعة صارِت تِدْعمُن بسّ يْكونوا بِحاجِة للمُساعدِة بِزِراعةْ البِسْتان والاِهْتِمام فيه.

[28:54]

From then on, Layal spent her life working with her husband Naji in the field, helping the needy. She learned her lesson—that she must not let her greed grow and should be content with what she has.

Naji also became more dedicated to the field, especially since the jar no longer gave them gold after what Layal had done. They were now forced to return to planting and harvesting crops in order to live and fulfill the jar's conditions by helping the poor.

With time, and after more than a year, life returned to the field. Greenery came back, and the harvest grew plentiful again. Naji and Layal worked in the field every day, caring for it and reaping its fruits. The field expanded and transformed from a small plot into a major source of food for many needy families in the village.

Naji and Layal discovered that their lives had become much happier than before, and their relationships with the people they were helping grew stronger. The whole village supported them whenever they needed help with planting and taking care of the field.

Arabic Text without Tashkeel

For a more authentic reading challenge, read the story without the aid of diacritics (tashkeel) and the parallel English translation.

جرة الفلاح

بضيعة صغيرة بالجبل، كان في شاب إسمو ناجي، عايش هو ومرتو ليال وبيو.

بهيدي الضيعة كانوا الناس عايشين حياة بسيطة ومتواضعة. بيزرعوا أرضن ويبخزنوا المونة لفصل الشتي حتى يقدروا يعيشوا أيام البرد والتلج. والناس بهيدي الضيعة كان عندن قناعة بطبيعة الحياة بالضيعة وكانوا عايشين حياتن التقليدية مبسوطين.

بيو لناجي كان كتير يحب الأرض. كان عندو بستان درة بيهتم فيه كتير. هيدا البستان كان مصدر العيش للعيلة كلا.

بيو لناجي بآخر فترة من عمرو مرض كتير، لحد ما في نهار كان وضعو الصحي كتير متدهور.

عيط لإبنو ناجي حتى يخبرو بوصيتو قبل ما يموت وقلو: "ناجي يا إبني، أنا وضعي الصحي كتير عم يتدهور وحاسس إنو يمكن هيدي تكون آخر أيام حياتي. كرمال هيك بدي وصيك يا إبني إنو تهتموا ببعض إنت وليال في حال أنا متت، وما تنسوا تهتموا بالبستان. هيدا البستان بيعنيلي كتير. قضيت كل حياتي عم بزرعو وعشنا كل هالعمر منو. وهيدا البستان ورتتو من جدك بس كنت شاب بعمرك وهلأ عم ورتك ياه لإلك. اعتني فيه وما تخليه يتبهدل لإن هالبستان رح يكون مصدر عيشك الوحيد إنت ومرتك ليال ورح يأمنلكن أكل لفصل الشتي."

تاني يوم الصبح فاق ناجي ولقى بيو ميت. زعل عليه كتير وصاروا هو وليال وحيدين من دون وجود بيو. ما في غيرن وغير بستان الدرة يلي ورتو ياه بيو كرمال يعيش منو هو ومرتو.

بستان الدرة يلي ورتو ناجي وليال كان يعطي محصول كتير كبير، بيكفين مونة لكل السنة. بس مع الوقت، ناجي ما كان يهتم بالبستان وما كان يعتني بشتل الدرة. لهيك من بعد سنة من موت بيو صار محصود البستان يتراجع بشكل كتير كبير ويقل عدد الدرة يلي فيه، لوقت بطلوا ليال وناجي يكفيهن لحتى ياكلوا ويخزنوا مونة لفصل الشتي.

ليال ما كانت تحب الشغل وكانت كتير تنق على ناجي كرمال يشتغل بالأرض ويهتم فيا، بس ناجي كان كسلان وما كان مهتم بالزراعة أبدا. كان كل الوقت عم يشكي من زراعة الأرض ومن الشغل فيا.

وبنفس الوقت ليال ما كانت تساعد ناجي وكانت بس تطلب منو هو يهتم بالبستان، لحد ما بقي البستان من دون اهتمام من قبل حدن وصارت حالة البستان كل يوم أسوأ من يوم.

في نهار كانت ليال كتير معصبة من الوضع ومن قلة المحصول، وصارت كتير تشكي من ناجي ومن عدم اهتمامو بالأرض.

وناجي كان كل الوقت ملتهي بالتلفون والإنترنت، لحد ما بلشت ليال تلح بالطلب على ناجي وقالتلو: "شيل هالتلفون من إيدك وحاجة تضيع وقتك على الإنترنت واللعب! قوم اهتم شوي بهالبستان أحسن ما بكرا نموت من الجوع!"

ناجي ضحك ضحكة باستهزاء ورد عليا وقال: "إنتي مفتكرة إنو المشكلة مني؟ إنو إذا أنا هلأ لعبت بالتلفون بيبس البستان؟ نحنا ما إلنا حظ بهالبستان ولو بدو يعطينا محصول زيادة كان عطانا. هيدا البستان منحوس، ما بدي ضيع وقتي بالشغل فيه." ورجع ناجي حمل تلفونو وبلش يلعب عليه.

نزعجت ليال من الرد تبع ناجي ومن عدم مبالاتو بالشغل بالأرض وبتحسين وضع البستان، وقالتلو بانزعاج: "إنت هيدا يلي شاطر فيه، تشيل اللوم عن حالك وما تتحمل المسؤولية. مقضى كل وقتك ع التلفون لعب وسوشال ميديا وتضييع وقت ع الفاضي. لو إنك سقيت البستان وهتميت فيه منيح كان هلأ عطانا محصول أكتر

وكنا أمنا مونة يلي بتكفينا لفصل الشتي وما كنا تبهدلنا. بكرا بفصل الشتي شو بدنا ناكل؟ من وين بدنا نجيب طحين وخبز في حال ما قدرنا هلأ نتمون من محصول البستان؟"

بس فعليا المشكلة ما كانت من البستان متل ما ناجي قال. المشكلة كانت إنو ناجي وليال ما كانوا عم يهتموا بالبستان وكان ناجي كل الوقت يلعب على التلفون ويقضي كل النهار على السوشال ميديا والإنترنت، وليال تشكي من ناجي من دون ما هي تشتغل كمان بالبستان. لهيدا السبب البستان بطل يعطين حصاد متل ما كان يعطين من قبل.

بس ليال ضلت تنق على ناجي وتشكي من تصرفاتو بالبيت لوقت طويل، لحد ما نزعج منا ومن الحديث وبطل قادر يتحمل ملاحظاتا، وقالا: "شو بدك ياني أعمل طيب؟ أصلا البستان ما في محصول والدرة الموجود ما بيعملنا شي وأكيد ما بيكفينا بالشتي، يعني إذا حصدناهن أو لأ هي ذاتا لإن الكمية كتير قليلة."

جاوبتو ليال وقالتلو: "قوم نزال جيب الدرة الموجود حتى لو قلال، واسقي الشتلات الصغار بلكي الشهر الجاي بيكبر وبيزيد المحصول شوي قبل ما يوصل فصل الشتي. بيضل أحسن من اللعب وتضييع الوقت على التلفون."

ناجي نزعج من ملاحظات ليال الكتيرة وقرر ينزل على البستان كرمال توقف الجدال معو حول هيدا الموضوع. أخد جرة كان جايبا جديد ونزل كرمال يعبي فيا الدرة.

وقت وصل على البستان شاف إنو الدرة الموجود قليل كتير وما بيعبي كعب الجرة حتى. لهيك قرر يرجع ع البيت من دون ما يجيب الدرة ومن دون ما يهتم بالبستان، وكان بحالة نفسية كتير تعبانة لإن ما عارف منين بدو يأمن الأكل والشرب للبيت.

هو وراجع من البستان، سمع صوت كتير غريب طالع من قلب الجرة وعم بيقلو بصوت واطي وهادي: "رجاع على البستان يا ناجي وحصود الدرة الموجود. حتى

لو كان في بس حبة وحدة أفضل من إنك تتركا. ممكن يجي يوم وتعتاز تاكل حبة درة وحدة."

ناجي ستغرب الصوت وخاف كتير. وصار يدور كرمال يعرف كيف طلع هيدا الصوت من قلب الجرة. وصار يتطلع بقلب الجرة يشوف إذا فيا شي، بس الجرة كانت فاضية.

بالأخير فكر حالو عم يتخايل الصوت من راسو وإنو الصوت مش حقيقي. بس بنفس الوقت قرر يسمع لهيدا الصوت الجاي من الجرة ورجع ع البستان كرمال يجيب الدرة.

بس رجع ناجي ع البستان، قطف الدرة الموجود وحطن بالجرة، وكانوا الدرة كتير قلال وما عبوا غير شوي من كعب الجرة.

هو وعم بيعبي وقع منو محبسو الدهب ونزل بقلب الجرة. وفجأة شاف ناجي كل حبات الدرة يلي بالجرة عم تلمع وتحولوا لدهب.

ورجع سمع نفس الصوت عم يحكيه من قلب الجرة مرة تانية، وقلو: "بما إنك قررت ترجع وتشتغل بالأرض وتقطف الدرة، هيدي الدرة تحولت لدهب. وصار فيك إنت ومرتك تبيعوهن وتعيشوا حياة كريمة من دون ما تعتازوا حدن. بس تذكر منيح إنو ما لازم حدا يعرف بهيدا الشي، وهيدا لازم يضل سر بيناتنا، وفي حال طمعت وصار بدك تخبي المصاري يلي منك بحاجتا رح تحل عليك وعلى مرتك لعنة الجرة."

ناجي نبسط كتير وكتشف إنو هيدي الجرة سحرية. بس رجع ع البيت، أخد قرار يسمع نصيحة الجرة وما يخبر حدن بالموضوع، ولا حتى مرتو ليال.

وقلا للجرة: "بوعدك إنو ما رح نطمع ورح نكتفي بالقدر يلي نحنا بحاجة لإلو كرمال نعيش وما نكون بحاجة. أكتر من هيك ما رح أطلب منك وما رح إسعى ليكون عندي دهب كتير. كل هدفي كون عم أمن أكل وشرب للبيت لإن من بعد ما مات بيي بطل عندي حدن والبستان بطل يعطينا محصود كفاية."

بعد فترة أسبوع لاحظت ليال إنو ناجي صار يجيب غراض على البيت أكتر من العادة، وستغربت منين عم يجيب المصاري ليدفع لكل هيدي الغراض.

وضلت ليال تسألو لناجي منين عم يجيب المصاري، بس هو ما كان يخبرا. وبليلة من الليالي ألحت ليال على ناجي مصرة إنو تعرف الحقيقة.

ساعتا ناجي قرر يخبرا بس طلب منا ما تخبر حدن. خبرا ناجي لليال شو صار معو وعن قصة الجرة، وفرجاها على الدرة يلي تحولوا وصاروا دهب.

ليال صارت تضحك والفرحة ما كانت سايعتا، وقالتلو لناجي: "هيدي الجرة رح تكون وسيلتنا لنصير أغنيا ونطلع من حياة الفقر يلي نحنا فيا. رح نشتري درة من السوق نبيعن فيا ونحولن لدهب ونبيعن. بهيدي الطريقة منصير أغنيا كتير بخلال سنة، منشتري قصر كبير وأرض تانية غير هيدي الأرض ومنفتح أكبر مزرعة بالبلد ومنتاجر بالمحصول تبعا."

ناجي ستغرب ردة فعل مرتو وخاف من الطمع يلي شافو بعيونا، وجاوبا: "يمكن ما لازم نطمع كتير يا ليال، هودي الدهب بيعيشونا سنة ونحنا ما بحاجة لمصاري أكتر من هيك. المهم نقدر نأمن أكلنا وشربنا. شوفي وضعنا قبل هلأ كيف كان وكيف صار. شو بدنا بزيادة المصاري إذا نحنا ما محتاجينا؟"

ليال ما قتنعت من ردة فعل ناجي وبقيت مصرة تنتج أكبر قدر ممكن من الدهب من خلال هيدي الجرة، وردت عليه: "هيدي فرصتنا الدهبية إنو نصير أغنيا ونجمع مصاري بيكفونا نعيش كل حياتنا بالنعيم وبقصر بدل هالبيت الصغير يلي نحنا فيه. ما لازم نضيع هيدي الفرصة من إيدنا."

جاوبا ناجي: "الجرة وقتا حولت الدرة لدهب حكيت معي وقالتلي إنو قدمتلنا الدهب لحتى نقدر ناكل ونعيش، بس مش لحتى نصير أغنيا ونترك بيتا. لهيك ما لازم نطمع ولازم نكتفي بالموجود لإن في حال ما كتفينا رح تحل علينا لعنة الجرة."

حاولت ليال تقنع ناجي بفكرتا بس هو بقي مصر إنو ما لازم يطمعوا ولازم يكتفوا بالموجود. لهيك قرر يشتري بالدهب درة وأكل وشرب للبيت.

وكمان قرر إنو يستعمل الجرة مرة وحدة بالسنة في حال عتازوا أكل وما كان معن مصاري كفاية، بهيدي الطريقة ما بيكون أخل بوعدو للجرة.

بس ليال ما حبت الفكرة وما قتنعت أبدا بموقف ناجي، وكان كل هدفا كيف بدا تصير غنية كتير وصارت تفكر كيف بدا تاخد الجرة حتى تعمل منا دهب ويصير معا مصاري أكتر.

بليلة من الليالي من عشية، فاتوا ليال وناجي تيناموا. وليال ما قدرت تنام وكان راسا مشغول بالجرة وبالدهب.

لهيك بس نام ناجي، شافتو ليال إنو غفي وإنو مش حاسس عليا، فقامت ليال بالليل وأخدت الجرة وخبتا بالقبو تحت البيت وحطت محلا جرة تانية متلا بالزبط، وبهيدي الطريقة ناجي ما رح يعرف بالموضوع ورح يفكر إنو الجرة الجديدة هي نفسا القديمة، وجرة الدهب الحقيقية صارت بإيد ليال ومخباية بالقبو من دون علم ناجي.

تاني يوم راح ناجي على السوق. باع الدهب يلي معو وشترى فين درة كرمال يزرع البستان من جديد، وشترى كمان أكل وشرب للبيت.

بس وصل ناجي، شافت ليال الدرة وشافت وين ضبن كرمال تاني يوم يقوم يزرعن بالبستان.

بعد نهار طويل، فاتوا ناجي وليال متل العادة تيناموا، وبس نام ناجي بالليل أخدت ليال قسم من الدرة يلي شتراهن ونزلت على القبو.

فتحت ليال الجرة وحطت فيا الدرة ورجعت حطت محبسا الدهب فوقن. نطرت ليال بشغف تتشوف كيف الدرة بدو يصير دهب.

وبالفعل تحولوا الدرة لدهب متل ما صار أول مرة مع ناجي. ليال نبسطت كتير إنو خطتا نجحت وصار معا دهب، وصار فيا تشتري درة أكتر وتحولن لدهب.

وقالت لنفسا: "وأخيرا رح يتحقق حلمي وصير غنية ويصير معي كتير مصاري. وأخيرا رح إشتري قصر كتير كبير وإطلع من هالبيت الصغير يلي عايشة فيه."

نسيت ليال شو قلا ناجي عن اللعنة يلي معقول تصيبن في حال طمعو، وكان كل هدفا تركيزا على كيف تعمل مصاري أكتر.

ليال صار معا دهب كتير وضلت على مدة شهر تشتري درة وتحولن لدهب، من بعدا تبيع الدهب وتخبي المصاري بخزنة عندا بالبيت.

بس هيدا الشي ما ضل لوقت كتير، لإن بيوم من الأيام فات ناجي لعند ليال ونتبه إنو صرلا فترة طويلة ما لابسة محبس الدهب تبعا، وستغرب كتير الموضوع لإن ليال كانت كل حياتا من بعد الزواج تلبس محبس الدهب وما تشلحو من إيدا.

كرمال هيك سألا ناجي لليال: "وين محبسك الدهب يلي كنتي دايما تلبسيه؟ صرلك فترة طويلة ما لابستيه، ضابتيه بشي مطرح بالبيت؟"

تلبكت ليال من السؤال وما عرفت كيف تجاوب، وصارت تجرب تألف حجج ومبررات حتى ناجي ما يعرف بالقصة المزبوطة حول جرة الدهب يلي خبتا ليال بالقبو.

وجاوبتو ليال لناجي وقالت: "ما بعرف وين بالزبط ضيعتو. كان بإيدي من فترة بس ما بعرف كيف ضاع. فجأة فقت من النوم وتطلعت بإيدي ولقيت المحبس ضاع. يمكن وقع بالأرض أو بالمطبخ، ويمكن ضاع بالبستان، ما بعرف وين موجود. وما كنت لاقيه. بس إنت ما تعتل هم. بكرا منلاقيه مش مشكلة. ما كتير تفكر بالموضوع."

ليال كانت كتير ملبكة هي وعم بتجاوبو لناجي وما عرفت تحكي منيح، وصارت تتلبك بالحكي وصار أحمر وجا من خوفا إنو ناجي يعرف بالحقيقة.

ناجي نتبه ولاحظ إنو في شي غريب صاير وإنو ليال عم تخبي شي عنو، وحس إنو ليال ما كانت عم تقول الحقيقة عن قصة المحبس.

من بعدا، قرر ناجي يراقب ليال بالسر من دون ما تحس عليه كرمال يكتشف شو مخبية عنو.

ومتل كل يوم، كانت ليال تنطر ناجي ليفوت ينام كرمال تنزل هي ع القبو وتحول الدرة لدهب، وتبيعن وتخبي المصاري بخزنة خبتا على تخيتة المطبخ.

وبليلة من الليالي فاتوا ليال وناجي كرمال يناموا، بس ناجي قرر هالمرة إنو يمثل على ليال ويعمل حالو نايم، لأنو حس إنو ليال ما عم بتنام قبل ما هو يغفى.

ناجي عمل حالو نايم وصار يراقب تحركات ليال تيشوف شو رح تعمل من بعدا. من بعد ١٠ دقايق، وبس شافت ليال إنو ناجي نام، قامت من التخت بالسر من دون ما تعمل أي صوت أو ضجة ونزلت متل العادة على القبو كرمال تحول الدرة لدهب.

هي ونازلة على القبو حس عليا ناجي وقام من التخت ولحقا من دون ما تحس عليه، ونزل وراها على القبو يلي تحت بيتن.

فتح ناجي باب القبو فتحة صغيرة من دون ما يعمل ضجة أو صوت، وشاف إنو ليال مخبية الجرة بالقبو وعم تحول الدرة لدهب بشكل سري من دون ما حدا يعرف بالموضوع. ناجي نزعج وخاف كتير من إنو تحل علين لعنة الجرة، وتذكر الحكي يلي قالتلو ياه الجرة بأول مرة حول فيا الدرة لدهب.

فتح الباب وفات على القبو، وقف حد ليال وقلا: "ليال شو عم تعملي هون؟ مش على أساس كنتي نايمة؟ شو نزلتي تعملي بالقبو بهيدا الوقت المتأخر من الليل؟ وهيدا شو يلي حدك؟" وأشار بإيدو على الجرة.

بس سمعت ليال ناجي عم يحكيا برمت وشافتو واقف حدا. نقزت ليال وتفاجئت من وجود ناجي بالقبو، لإن كل فكرا إنو ناجي كان نايم وما شافا نزلت، من بعدا برمت ليال بسرعة كبيرة وكان بدا تخبي الجرة وراها كرمال ناجي ما يشوفا.

ومن كتر السرعة بالحركة والارتباك من الموقف يلي صار معا، ضربت ليال إجرا بالجرة وزحطت ووقعت جواتا وصارت تطلب المساعدة من ناجي.

ركض ناجي لعندا كرمال يساعدا تطلع من قلب الجرة، وفجأة بيلاقي إنو ليال تحولت لدهب وصارت جماد وبطل فيا تتحرك. كان بعدا قادرة بس تحكي.

ناجي خاف كتير من الشي يلي صار مع ليال وبلش يجرب يلاقي طريقة كيف ممكن ترجع ليال لحالتا الطبيعية، بس للأسف ما قدر يعمل أي شي لأن ليال تحولت لدهب.

مرة جديدة بيطلع الصوت نفسو من قلب الجرة، بس هيدي المرة كان غاضب ومزعوج كتير من تصرفات ناجي وليال، وقلا لليال: "طمعك يا ليال خلاكي توقعي بالجرة وتتحولي لدهب، وهلأ ما بقى ينفعك كل المصاري يلي خبيتيا. ما كتفيتي بالقليل وصار بدك تراكمي ثروتك وتجمعي مصاري منك بحاجة لإلا. هلأ صرتي إنتي بنفسك دهب، والطريقة الوحيدة لإنك ترجعي متل ما كنتي من قبل، هي إنو تقضي كل بقية عمرك عم تزرعي درة وتوزعين على الناس الفقرا والمحتاجين، وفي حال مرق نهار واحد من دون ما تساعدي فيه الناس، رح ترجعي لدهب. وبنفس الوقت كل المصاري يلي خبيتيا بالخزنة رح تختفي، وكل الدهب يلي خبيتيه رح يتحول مرة جديدة لدرة."

وكمان حكيت الجرة مع ناجي وقالتلو: "وإنت يا ناجي، وعدتني إنك ما رح تخبر حدن وما رح تطمعوا بالدهب، ورجعت خبرت ليال وصار بدا تعمل مصاري أكتر من حاجتا. هيدا يلي صار بمرتك ليال هو لعنة الجرة يلي خبرتك عنا وحذرتك منا. هلأ حل المشكلة صار بين إيديكن وإنتو رح تدفعوا تمن الأخطاء يلي عملتوها."

ناجي وليال ما كان عندن خيار تاني غير إنو تقبل ليال بهيدي الشروط يلي قالتلا هي الجرة، أو بتضلا كل بقية عمرا قطعة دهب ما فيا تتحرك وما فيا تمشي.

وافقت ليال على شروط الجرة، ورجعت لطبيعتا وختفى الدهب عن جسما وصار فيا تتحرك.

وضلت ليال كل حياتا عم تشتغل مع زوجا ناجي بالبستان وتساعد الناس المحتاجة، وتعلمت ليال درس إنو ما لازم تزيد طمعا ولازم ترضى بحاجاتا من دون ما تطمع أكتر.

وناجي صار يهتم أكتر بالبستان لأن الجرة ما عاد تعطين دهب من بعد يلي عملتو ليال، وصاروا مجبورين يرجعوا يزرعوا الأرض ويحصدوها حتى يقدروا يعيشوا وينفذوا شروط الجرة ويساعدوا الناس الفقرا.

مع الوقت وبعد أكتر من سنة، رجعت الحياة والخضار على البستان ورجع المحصود يزيد ويكتر، وصاروا ليال وناجي كل يوم يهتموا بالأرض ويعتنوا فيا ويحصدوا الحصاد، وصار البستان أكبر بكتير وتحول من بستان صغير، لمصدر عيش عدد كبير من العيل المحتاجة بالضيعة.

وكتشفوا ليال وناجي إنو صارت حياتن سعيدة أكتر من قبل وصارت علاقتن بالناس يلي عم يساعدوهن أقوى، وكل الضيعة صارت تدعمن بس يكونوا بحاجة للمساعدة بزراعة البستان والاهتمام فيه.

Comprehension Questions

1. ويْن كان عايِش ناجي ومرْتو لَيال وبيّو؟

2. شو كان مصْدر رِزِق العيْلِة الوَحيد؟

3. شو صار مع بيّو لْناجي؟

4. شو كانِت وَصيِّةْ البيّ لْناجي قبِل ما يْموت؟

5. ليْش تْراجع محْصول البِسْتان بعْد موْت البيّ؟

6. كيف حُصِل ناجي على الجرّة السِّحْرية؟

7. شو صار بسّ وِقع محْبس ناجي بِالْجرّة؟

8. شو كان شرْط الجرّة لْناجي؟

9. شو عِمْلِت لَيال لمّا عِرْفِت عن سِرّ الجرّة؟

10. كيف سرقِت لَيال الجرّة مِن ناجي؟

11. شو كانِت خُطّةْ لَيال مع الجرّة؟

12. كيف عِرِف ناجي إنّو لَيال سرقِت الجرّة؟

13. شو صار مع لَيال لمّا وِقْعِت بِالْجرّة؟

14. شو كانِت شروط الجرّة كِرْمال لَيال تِرْجع لطبيعِتا؟

15. شو صار بِالْمصاري يَلّي خبّتا لَيال؟

16. كيف تْغيّرِت حَياةْ لَيال وناجي بعْد هَيْدي الحادْثِة؟

17. شو صار بِالْبِسْتان بعْد ما رِجْعوا يِهْتمّوا فيه؟

18. مين كان يْساعِد لَيال وناجي بِالْبِسْتان؟

19. شو كان الدّرِس يَلّي تْعلّمِتو لَيال مِن هَيْدي القُصّة؟

20. كيف صار البِسْتان مصْدر رِزِق لكِلّ الضّيْعة؟

1. Where did Naji live with his wife Layal and father?
2. What was the family's only source of income?
3. What happened to Naji's father?
4. What was the father's will to Naji before he died?
5. Why did the field's harvest decline after the father's death?
6. How did Naji get the magical jar?
7. What happened when Naji's ring fell into the jar?
8. What was the jar's condition for Naji?
9. What did Layal do when she learned about the jar's secret?
10. How did Layal steal the jar from Naji?
11. What was Layal's plan with the jar?
12. How did Naji discover that Layal had stolen the jar?
13. What happened to Layal when she fell into the jar?
14. What were the jar's conditions for Layal to return to normal?
15. What happened to the money that Layal had hidden?
16. How did Layal and Naji's life change after this incident?
17. What happened to the field after they started taking care of it again?
18. Who helped Layal and Naji with the field?
19. What lesson did Layal learn from this story?
20. How did the field become a source of income for the whole village?

Answers to the Comprehension Questions

1. كانوا عايْشين بِضَيْعة صْغيرِة بِالجّبل.

2. كان بِسْتان الدُّرة مصْدر رِزْقُن الوَحيد.

3. مرِض كْتير ومات.

4. وَصّاه يِهْتمّ بِالبِسْتان لأنّو مصْدر عيْشُن الوَحيد.

5. لإنّو ناجي ما كان يِهْتمّ بِالبِسْتان وكان مِلْتِهي بِالتِّلِفوْن.

6. كان عِنْدو جرّة جْديدِة وصارِت سِحْرية لمّا وِقع فيا محْبسو.

7. تْحوّل الدُّرة يَلّي بِالجرّة لدهب.

8. ما يْكون طمّاع وما يْخبِّر حدا عن سِرّ الجرّة.

9. سرقِت الجرّة وخبّتا بِالْقبو.

10. نطْرِت لحتّى نام ناجي وبدّلِت الجرّة بْوِحْدِة تانْية.

11. كان بدّا تْحوّل كِلّ الدُّرة لدهب وتْصير غنية كْتير.

12. لاحظ إنّو ما عاد في محْبسا وراقبا بِاللّيْل.

13. تْحوّلِت لتِمْثال دهب.

14. لازِم تْساعِد الفُقرا وتِزْرع الدُّرة كِلّ حَياتا.

15. تْحوّل كِلّو لدُرة.

16. صاروا يِشْتِغلوا سَوا بِالْبِسْتان ويْساعْدوا النّاس.

17. كْبِر البِسْتان وصار يَعْطي محْصول كْتير.

18. كِلّ أهْل الضّيْعة صاروا يْساعْدوُن.

19. إنّو الطّمع مِش مْنيح ولازِم تِكْتِفي بِحاجاتا.

20. صار البِسْتان كْبير كْتير ويَعْطي رِزِق لكِلّ العيّل الفقيرة.

1. They lived in a small village in the mountains.

2. The cornfield was their only source of income.

3. He became very ill and died.

4. He instructed him to take care of the field as it was their only source of livelihood.

5. Because Naji neglected the field and was distracted by his phone.

6. He had a new jar that became magical when his ring fell into it.

7. The corn in the jar turned into gold.

8. Not to be greedy and not to tell anyone about the jar's secret.

9. She stole the jar and hid it in the basement.

10. She waited until Naji was asleep and replaced the jar with another one.

11. She wanted to turn all the corn into gold to become very wealthy.

12. He noticed her ring was missing and watched her at night.

13. She turned into a golden statue.

14. She had to help the poor and grow corn for the rest of her life.

15. It all turned back into corn.

16. They started working together in the field and helping people.

17. The field grew larger and produced more crops.

18. All the villagers began helping them.

19. That greed is bad and she should be content with what she needs.

20. The field became very large and provided income for all the poor families.

Summary

Read the scrambled summary of the story below. Write the correct number (1–10) in the blank next to each event to show the proper sequence.

_____ ناجي كان عايِش مع مرْتو لَيال وبِيّو بِضَيْعة صْغيرِة، وكان عِنْدُن بِسْتان دُرة.

_____ وِقع محْبس ناجي بِالْجرّة وتْحوّلِت الدُّرة لدهب.

_____ قِبْلِت لَيال شُروط الجرّة إنّا تْساعِد الفُقرا وتِزْرع الدُّرة.

_____ مِرِض بيّو ومات، بعْد ما وَصّى ناجي يِهْتمّ بِالبِسْتان.

_____ وِقْعِت لَيال بِالْجرّة وتْحوّلِت لدهب.

_____ كْبِر البِسْتان وصار يْساعِد كِلّ العيَل الفقيرة بِالضَّيْعة.

_____ تْراجع محْصول البِسْتان لإِنّو ناجي ما كان يِهْتمّ في.

_____ صارِت لَيال تِسْتعْمِل الجرّة كِلّ ليْلِة وتْخبّي المصاري.

_____ خبّر ناجي لَيال عن سِرّ الجرّة، ولَيال سرقِت الجرّة وخبّتا بِالْقبو.

_____ عْرِف ناجي عن السِّرّ وراقب لَيال بِاللّيْل.

Key to the Summary

1   Naji lived with his wife Layal and father in a small village, owning a cornfield.

4   Naji's ring fell into the jar and turned the corn into gold.

9   Layal accepted the jar's conditions to help the poor and grow corn.

2   The father fell ill and died, after instructing Naji to care for the field.

8   Layal fell into the jar and turned into gold.

10   The field grew and helped all the poor families in the village.

3   The field's harvest declined because Naji neglected it.

6   Layal began using the jar every night and hiding money.

5   Naji told Layal about the jar's secret, so she stole it and hid it in the basement.

7   Naji discovered the secret and watched Layal at night.

Levantine Arabic Readers Series

www.lingualism.com/lar

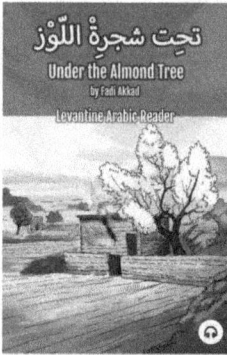

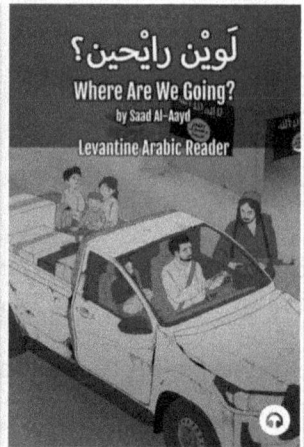

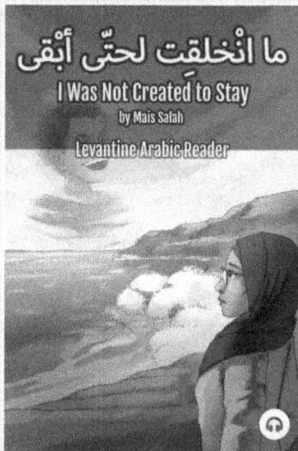

تحِت شجرةِ اللّوز
Under the Almond Tree
by Fadi Akkad
Levantine Arabic Reader

البتْرا
Petra
by Raed Bader
Levantine Arabic Reader

Levantine Arabic Reader
اللي بيزْرع بيْحْصُد
Where There's a Will
by Ahmed Younis

ما انْخلقِت لحتّى أبْقى
I Was Not Created to Stay
by Mais Salah
Levantine Arabic Reader

لوَيْن رايْحين؟
Where Are We Going?
by Saad Al-Aayd
Levantine Arabic Reader

وَرقةِ اليانصيب
The Lottery Ticket
by Serj D.
Levantine Arabic Reader

قدّيْش حقّ السّمك؟
How Much is the Fish?

خليل و الأكْوان المتعدّدة
Khalil and the Multiverse

شابّ طموح
An Ambitious Young Man

عبْد العزيز جاسم
Dear Abdul Aziz

القاتل الأكْبر
The Worst Killer

سِتّات بيروت
The Girls of Beirut

جرّةِ الفلّاح
The Farmer's Jar
by Mona Noureddine
Levantine Arabic Reader

رجْعةِ المدارِس
Back to School
by Raed Bader
Levantine Arabic Reader

حَياةِ فاطْمة
Fatimah's Life
by Israa Ramadan
Levantine Arabic Reader